FOLK PLAYS
FOR PUPPETS
YOU CAN MAKE

Written and illustrated by
TOM TICHENOR

Nashville   ABINGDON PRESS   New York

Ref,
j 791.53
T

ISBN 0-687-13239-8

To Poindexter and his friends

Contents

How to Give a Puppet Play

A puppet play is a play that is made to be used with puppets. Puppets take the parts of people or of animals in the play.

In a puppet play, puppets act like people. Even if the puppets are taking the parts of animals, they often talk and do all the things that people do.

But a puppet play is not just like any other play. In real life, or in a play that is made for people to act in, we learn many things about each person we see. We see that each person can sometimes be good, and sometimes bad. Sometimes they can be happy, and sometimes sad. And we can see that each person can be and do many different things.

But in a puppet play, we learn only one or two things about the puppet in the play. The puppet does not change from being a good puppet to being a bad puppet and then to being a good puppet as a real person can. And a puppet is not wise in some things and foolish in others. He is either a wise puppet or a foolish puppet all the way through the play.

A puppet in your plays should never be just a little sad, or a little happy, or a little bad. If he is sad, he is very sad. If he is happy, he is very, very happy. And if he is bad, he is very, very bad.

The plays in this book were made to be used with puppets. On the next few pages, you will find some ways of making puppets that you can use with your plays.

But you can act in these plays yourself, too. When you act in them, just think that they were made for puppets. If you are playing a sad part, be very, very sad. If you are playing a bad man, be very, very bad. Try to act just as a puppet would act if a puppet were taking the part.

At the beginning of each play you will find a list of the people or animals who are in the play. After each name you will find a few words about that person or animal. This will help you to know how you or your puppet should act.

When you have used all of the puppet plays in this book, you may want to make some plays of your own. Choose a story that you think will make a good puppet play and try to write a puppet play for it.

How to Make Puppets

There are many ways to make a puppet. The easiest kind of puppet to make is a paper puppet. To make a paper puppet, you must first decide what your puppet should look like. Is it a man, a woman, or a child? If it is a man, is it a fat man, or a thin man? Is it a tall man, or a short man? Or do you need an animal puppet? If so, what kind of animal do you need?

When you know what kind of puppet you need, you can cut a picture that looks like the puppet you want out of a magazine or newspaper. Or you can draw a picture of the kind of puppet you want to use in your play.

When the picture is cut out, paste it on a piece of cardboard. Then cut the figure out of the cardboard. Paste a long stick of wood or a strip of heavy cardboard to the back of the puppet. If you like, you can give your puppet a cloth costume. Or you can leave it just as it is.

You can use your puppet by getting in back of your puppet stage and holding the puppet up from behind so that the people who are watching the play can see the puppet but cannot see you.

Paper puppets are fun to use. But after you have used them for a while

you may want a different kind of puppet. You may need a puppet that can do more things than a paper puppet can do. You may want a puppet, perhaps, that can pick things up. Then you will want a hand puppet.

To make a hand puppet, you will need, first of all, a piece of cloth the size of a handkerchief. Cut three holes in the handkerchief. The holes should be in a straight line. When you use the puppet, your first finger goes into the middle hole. This finger will hold the puppet's head. Your thumb and your middle finger go into the other

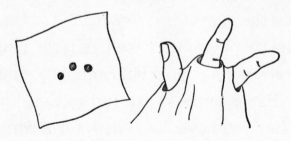

two holes. They are the puppet's hands.

The head of the puppet can be made of heavy paper. You can use newspaper, wrapping paper, or kitchen toweling. Roll a long strip of the paper around your first finger and fasten the end with a piece of tape. Fasten

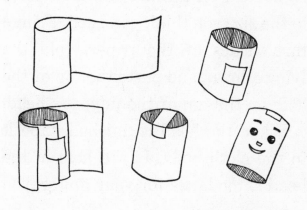

the inside with tape, too, so that you can get your finger back into the head again.

Now that you have shaped the head, you can make it look like anything you want it to look like. Cover the rolled paper with crepe-paper if you wish to give it the right skin color.

Then glue on, or draw on, eyes, nose, and a mouth. These can be bits of colored paper.

A scrap of fur or a few pieces of yarn cut the right length and tied together in the middle will do very nicely for hair. Or you can make paper hair, too. Choose a piece of paper the right color for the hair and cut it down to the size you think you need. Fringe three sides of the paper, fold the fringe down, and paste the top of the hair on the top of the puppet's head.

When the head is finished, tape it to the cloth body. If the hole in the head is too large for your finger, you

can put some cotton inside the hole to make it fit right.

Some puppets you will see in this book are made entirely of cloth. Their heads are two round pieces of cloth sewed together and stuffed with cotton. The eyes, nose, and mouth are pieces of cloth sewed on or else they are embroidered on with thread or yarn. The hair is made of yarn and is

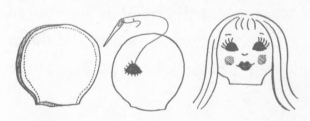

sewed on. A puppet made of cloth will last a long, long time.

When you have your puppets, you will need a stage for them to act on. To make a simple stage, put two chairs about three feet apart. You can use armchairs with arms about the same height. Or you can use straight-backed chairs that are straight across the top or that have straight boards or rungs across the back.

If you are using armchairs, place a board or a heavy piece of cardboard across the arms of the chairs. If you are using straight-backed chairs, face the chairs toward each other. Place the board across the tops of the chairs or across the rungs in the back of the chairs, whichever height is best for you.

Next, cover the front of your stage with a large towel or cloth. Get down on your knees behind it. The stage

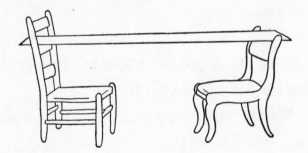

should be just above your head. If you are using the straight chairs, the seats of the chairs will make a good place for you to place your script while you read it.

If you want scenery for your play, you can use a large cardboard box for a background. Cut off any flaps at the top of the box. Face the opening toward the audience. Place the front end of what is now the bottom of the box on the board you are using for the base of your stage. The back end of the box should extend over the back of the board. Now cut out the part of the bottom of the box that lies behind the board so you can put your puppets up through the floor of the stage. It will

be best if you leave a small strip of the bottom of the box at the back of the hole. You can put some scenery on this space.

Paint any scenery you like on the back of the box. Or make scenery on another piece of paper and fasten it in with tape so that you can change it when you need to.

You can also make paper houses, trees, or any other stage props you need for the play.

Make a simple curtain for your box stage, too. Take a piece of material or crepe-paper as long as the stage and a little bit higher. Make a hem at the top. Run a wire through the hem and fasten the wire across the top of the box. Now you have a curtain that you can pull back and forth with your hand.

Now you are ready to give a puppet play.

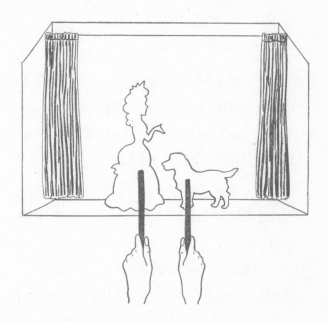

The Three Billy Goats Gruff

CHARACTERS

BILLY GOAT GRUFF: A big, old goat, with long horns. He talks very loudly about the things he is going to do.

MOTHER GOAT GRUFF: A smaller goat than Billy. She talks softly and slowly. She is shy, but will do anything to keep Baby Goat Gruff out of trouble.

BABY GOAT GRUFF: A small goat, with small horns. He makes up his mind to do something, and he does it.

MRS. RACCOON: If something has never been done, she is sure that it will never be done. And she says so in a very loud voice.

20

MR. BEAVER: He always goes ahead and does the thing that he thinks needs to be done.

TROLL: A mean old dwarf.

SCENERY

All the scenery you really need is a bridge. You can make a bridge railing out of paper. If you are using a board for your stage, fasten the railing to the back of the board. If you are using a cardboard box, fasten the bridge to the front of the opening in the bottom of your stage.

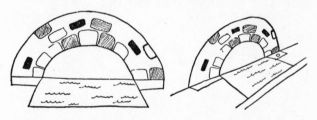

If you wish, you can make it look as though water is running under the bridge. Use blue paper for water.

If you are using a box stage, the scenery in the background may show the stream going off in the distance.

One side of the stream should be bare. The other side of the stream should have nice green grass.

ACTION

At the start of the play, all of the puppets should be on one side of the stage—the bare side. You can make your characters cross the bridge just by moving them past the bridge. The Troll can come up in back of the puppets crossing the bridge. This will make it look as though the Troll is on the far side of the bridge.

PLAY

BILLY: Mother Goat Gruff!

MOTHER: What do you want, Billy Goat Gruff?

BILLY: There is no grass on this side of the stream. There is no grass at all. So I am going to think of a way for us to get some grass. I am going to think of a way for us to cross the stream.

MOTHER: Do you think you can? Do you think there is a way for us to cross?

(BABY GRUFF *comes running up.*)

BABY: Mother! Mother Goat Gruff!

MOTHER: What is it, Baby Goat Gruff?

BABY: I'm hungry.

BILLY: We're all hungry. You are not the only one who is. I am going to think of a way to cross the stream. Then we can all go across to the green grass on the other side.

MOTHER: I wish there were a way to cross. But I don't know what it would be. That awful troll!

BABY: Will the troll get us if we cross the bridge? The troll is in the water.

MOTHER: Hush, Baby Goat Gruff. Don't think of going over the bridge. Don't ever try to do it. The troll will eat you up if you do.

BILLY: Now see here, Mother Goat Gruff. Don't make the baby afraid. I will see that we get across.

MOTHER: Oh, no, no. We must never cross the bridge.

MRS. RACCOON (*walking quickly up to the group*): What's that about the bridge? Of course you will never cross the bridge. The troll will keep

you from crossing. But I do wish there were more to eat on this side.

BILLY: Don't give up hope. We'll get across. I'll think of a way for us to cross. Of course we'll get to the other side.

MOTHER: Oh, no. I won't cross. And Baby Goat Gruff won't cross either.

MRS. RACCOON: We will never get to the other side.

MR. BEAVER (*walking slowly up to the others*): What's this? You won't

go across the bridge? Why won't you go, if you want to go?

MRS. RACCOON: A troll guards the bridge. You know the troll is there.

MR. BEAVER: Well, I might not like the idea of crossing the bridge.

But if I lived here, I would go over it if I wanted to. Good day.

(MR. BEAVER *walks slowly away*.)

BABY: I'm hungry. I want some nice green grass to eat. I want to cross the bridge.

MOTHER: No. no. You must not.

MRS. RACCOON: You will never cross the bridge.

BABY: I can. And I'm going to.

MOTHER: Baby, you must not. Oh, you must not.

BILLY: Wait a bit now. I will think of a way to cross the bridge. Let me think of a way.

BABY: I'm going now.

MOTHER: Wait! Wait Baby Goat Gruff!

BILLY: Yes, wait. Wait until I think of a way.

BABY: No. I'm going to cross the bridge, and I'm going to cross it now.

(*He sets out toward the bridge.*)

MOTHER: Wait, Baby Gruff. Wait for me.

(BABY *starts across the bridge.*)

TROLL: Who crosses over my stream?

BABY: I'm Baby Goat Gruff.

TROLL: I'm going to catch you, and I'm going to eat you.

BABY: Don't eat me. There is another goat coming who is bigger than I.

TROLL: A bigger goat? A bigger goat would make a bigger dinner.

BABY: And now I'm across the stream, just as I said I would be.

MOTHER: Oh, dear, Baby Goat Gruff. Wait right there until I come.

BILLY: He should have waited until I thought of a way to get us across. Don't you cross, too, Mother Goat Gruff. Wait. I'll think of a way for us to cross.

MOTHER: I must go after Baby.

(*She starts across the bridge.*)

TROLL: Who crosses over my stream?

MOTHER: It's only Mother Goat Gruff.

TROLL: I'm going to catch you, and I'm going to eat you.

MOTHER: Please don't eat me. I must get to Baby Goat Gruff. One who is bigger than I is coming soon. He's coming when he thinks of a way.

TROLL: A bigger goat? A bigger goat would make a bigger dinner. When is he coming?

BILLY: I'm coming now. I have found a way to cross the bridge. And I am going to cross.

28

(*He starts across the bridge.*)

TROLL: Who crosses over my stream?

BILLY: It's Billy Goat Gruff! And I will cross over.

TROLL: I'm going to catch you, and I'm going to eat you.

BILLY: I have found a way to cross. You can't stop me now. Come up and try if you like.

(TROLL *comes up out of the stream.* BILLY *butts him back into the stream.*)

TROLL: Ohhhhh. Ohhhhhh. Yes, I guess you can cross if you like.

BILLY: Yes, and now that I have found a way to cross, I will cross more often.

TROLL: Ohhhhh. Yes, I guess you will. I guess you will.

MRS. RACCOON (*still on the other side of the bridge*): I never would have believed it.

BILLY: Yes, I have found a way to cross the stream.

(*He goes the rest of the way across.*)

MOTHER: Oh, Billy, I am so glad.

MRS. RACCOON (*starting across the bridge*): But it was not Billy who found the way across. It was Baby Goat Gruff who found the way.

BABY: Yes, I crossed over first. I wanted to come over, and I came.

BILLY: But I found a way to take care of the troll. And now, let me show you where the grass is best. Just follow me. I can always find the best way.

(*All start up the hill.*)

The Princess Who Could Not Cry

CHARACTERS

PRINCESS GAY: A small girl who wears a crown. She laughs all of the time and talks in a laughing voice.

KING: He wears a crown. He does not like to laugh at all. He speaks in a stern voice.

PAGE: A small boy. He does everything that is asked of him. When he speaks, he talks softly.

MRS. WEST: She is a large woman. She does not look or act very happy.

GENERAL STRONG: A big man in a fancy suit. He talks very loudly.

MR. RAY: He looks very nice. When he talks he has something to say. But he does not talk in a loud voice.

GIRL: A small girl in an old dress. She carries a basket. She is shy.

SCENERY

Acts 1, 2, 4, and 5 take place in the Throne Room. All you need to make is a throne. Use a small box to make the seat of the throne. Paste a back to one side of the box. You can cover your throne with a cloth, if you like. Put the throne to one side of your stage.

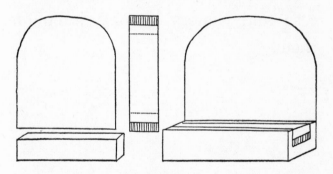

If you are using a box stage, you may want to add some fancy trimmings to the Throne Room. Try some cloth drapes at the back, or make anything else you think the Throne Room

might have in it to make it look fine.

Act 3 takes place in the Princess' playroom. All you need for your stage in this scene are some toys. Cut some toys out of paper. Cut them double so that they will stand up until the Princess and General Strong jump on them.

ACTION

If you want to use paper puppets for this play, you may want to fix them a little differently. Your King will have to sit on this throne part of the time. If you place the throne at one side of the stage in front of you, fold the King's body at the hips and at the knees so that he can sit. Instead of fastening a strip of cardboard or a piece of wood to the back of the King, fasten to the back of his head a piece of cardboard or a wire that will bend

easily. Bend the wire or fold the cardboard so that you can move the King, as he sits in his chair, from your place below the back of the stage.

The other puppets in this play will not need to sit down. But they will need to move out onto the board or stage in front of you. They will need to walk over to the King.

Your puppet will move onto the

stage if you use a piece of wire that is easily bent or a strong piece of cardboard to move it about with. Fasten part of the wire or strip of cardboard to the back of the puppet—fasten it firmly to the head as the picture shows.

Now bend the wire or fold the cardboard back above the fastening. The wire or cardboard should come straight back. At a place four or five inches from the puppet's head, bend the wire or fold the cardboard again. The wire or cardboard should come down so that you can move the puppet from below.

This puppet can now move about on your stage. The Princess and the General can even jump up and down on the toys in the playroom.

ACT I

GAY: Ha! Ha! Ha!

KING: Ah, good morning, Princess Gay.

GAY: Morning, Father. Isn't it a funny day? Ha! Ha! Ha!

KING: A funny day? What do you mean by a funny day?

GAY: The sun is laughing at us, and so is the wind. Can't you hear them? Oh, it is a funny day.

KING: My dear, you must learn that not all things are funny.

GAY: Ha! Ha! Ha!

KING: We are having visitors today. I hope that you will try not to laugh at them.

GAY: I'll try not to. But you know how I am. Ha! Ha! Ha!

KING: Yes, I'm afraid I do.

PAGE (*bowing before* KING): Mrs. West is here, sir.

KING: Show her in at once. And Princess, you are not to laugh at Mrs. West.

GAY: I'll try, Father. (*Laughs.*)

KING: Ah, Mrs. West. Do come in. What is it that you wish?

WEST: I must see you about my hat. My hat is new and—

GAY: (*Laughs.*)

WEST: Did I say something funny? What was it that I said?

KING: You said nothing funny, Mrs. West. Please go on. Gay will not laugh again.

WEST: I must see you about my hat. The hat is new, and I just saw Mrs. Winter with one like it. I want you to make a law——

GAY: (*Laughs again.*)

WEST: It's not funny. It's not funny at all.

GAY: (*Laughs very hard.*)

WEST: Well, now I know that what I hear is true. The Princess does laugh at everything. Good-by! (MRS. WEST *leaves.*)

KING: Princess, do you see what your laughing has done? Mrs. West has gone.

GAY: I'm sorry.

KING: Go to your room at once, and stay there until I send for you.

GAY: Yes, Father. Funny old room! Ha! Ha! Ha!

(PRINCESS *leaves*.)

KING: Page!

PAGE: Yes, sir!

KING: Something must be done about the Princess. Mr. Ray is the wisest man in the kingdom. Have him come to me at once.

ACT 2

(*Throne Room.* KING *and* MR. RAY *are talking*.)

KING: Mr. Ray, I have sent for you today ——

RAY: Yes, yes, because of the Prin-

cess. I have come because of her.

KING: Yes, the Princess——

RAY: Laughs all the time. I have worked and worked to find out why this is. And at last I may know why.

KING: Why is it, then?

RAY: The Princess is under a spell.

KING: Under a spell?

RAY: Yes, under a spell.

KING: What can be done for the spell? Is there something that we can do?

RAY: Yes, yes, there is something.

KING: Well, what is it then?

RAY: The Princess must be made to cry. If she cries just once, the spell will end. Then she will be just like everyone else. She will laugh when she is happy, and cry when she is sad.

KING: We must make her cry at once. We cannot hurt her in any way. But we must make her cry. Do you know how to do this, Mr. Ray?

RAY: No, no, I haven't had time to think of that yet. But someone in your kingdom should know a way.

KING: Someone in the kingdom! Someone in the palace would be better. Page!

PAGE: Yes, sir.

KING: Call General Strong.

PAGE: Yes, sir.

(*He disappears and returns in a short time with* GENERAL STRONG.)

KING: General Strong, we must find a way to make the Princess cry. It

seems to me that you should know a way.

GENERAL: Let me think, now. (*Thinks.*) You might shut the Princess up in a room by herself. If you would shut her up for a week, she would surely cry.

KING: This sounds like a strong way of doing things. But we will see. We will see.

ACT 3

(*The* PRINCESS' *playroom.* KING *and* GENERAL STRONG *are there.*)

KING: Well, the Princess will soon be here. I do hope that she will be crying when she comes.

(PRINCESS *comes in.*)

GAY (*laughing*) : Hello, Father.

KING: Princess Gay, how can you laugh after a week by yourself?

GAY: I like myself. And it was a funny old room. (*Laughs.*)

KING: One week in a room by herself, and still she cannot cry. General, do you have any other ideas?

GENERAL: I may have. I can see that the Princess enjoys her toys.

KING: Of course she does. She has many fine toys.

GENERAL: Then let me break her toys. Breaking her toys will make her cry.

KING: Break her toys? Oh, no, no! It makes me cry to think of it.

GENERAL: Then it will make the Princess cry.

KING: Try it, then. Look, Princess.

GENERAL: Yes, look at me, Princess. I will jump up and down upon your toys.

(GENERAL *jumps up and down on the toys on the floor.*)

44

KING: Oh, I cannot watch this.

GAY: I can. It looks like fun. (*Laughs.*) Let me help you.

KING: Not even this will work.

ACT 4

(*Throne room again.* KING *and* MR. RAY *are talking.* GENERAL *stands near the throne.*)

KING: I have called you again, as you see.

RAY: Yes, yes. The Princess still cannot cry.

KING: Everyone in the palace has tried to make her cry. But no one can do it.

RAY: Ask the people of your kingdom. Someone will know a way.

KING: Very well. We will ask the people of the kingdom. Page! Page!

PAGE: Yes, sir.

KING: Let all of the people know that we must make the Princess cry. And —yes—and to anyone who can do it, I will give ten golden coins.

PAGE: Yes, sir. I will let them know at once, sir.

ACT 5

(*Throne room again.* KING *is on throne.* GENERAL *is near by.*)

PAGE: A girl is here, sir.

KING: A girl? Did you say a girl?

PAGE: Yes, sir. A girl with a basket, sir.

KING: Very well. Have her come in.

PAGE: This way.

(*Goes to door; brings girl in.*)

GIRL: I have come at your call, O King! I have come to make the Princess cry.

KING: To make the Princess cry! What can you do? All of the wise men in the kingdom have not been able to make the Princess cry.

GIRL: Yes, sir. But if I may see the Princess——

KING: Very well. Everyone else has tried. You may as well try, too. Page, show her to the Princess.

GIRL: May I take my basket?

KING: Yes, of course. Of course you may take your basket.

(GIRL *goes out, following* PAGE.)

KING: Now what does she think she can do?

PAGE: (*returning*) I don't know, sir. But don't you hear a noise?

(*Crying is heard from other room.*)

KING: Can that be the Princess? Can the Princess be crying?

(PRINCESS *runs into room.* GIRL *follows.*)

GAY: Father, I am crying. I can't help it. I am crying.

KING: Wonderful! Wonderful! And how did this come about?

GIRL: I cut open an onion.

KING: You cut open an onion? Of course! Why didn't I think of that?

PAGE: Why didn't I?

GENERAL: And why didn't I?

KING: The ten golden coins are yours, my girl. They will buy many onions. But it is worth many onions to me to see the Princess cry.

The City Mouse and the Country Mouse

CHARACTERS

HIRAM MOUSE: A brown mouse. He is friendly to everyone.

CHARLIE MOUSE: A gray mouse. He likes excitement and danger.

COOK: A fat woman with an apron. She is often very angry.

DOG and CAT.

SCENERY

Act 1 takes place in a barn. If you have a little hay or straw, place it on your stage. If you cannot get hay or straw, cut long, narrow pieces of yellow paper and lay them on your stage.

There might be a pile of straw at one side of the stage. Hiram can be hidden behind this pile at the start of the first act.

If you are using a box stage, you might suggest walls and the ceiling of a barn on the top and sides of the

box. Find a picture of a barn to help you. You might also suggest a door at one side. Charlie can come up on this side as though he has come through the door.

In the second act you will want to have a house. You need have only one room. For chairs, see the directions for making a throne in "The Princess Who Could Not Cry." A table can be made out of a box, also. Use just the top or the bottom of the box. Turn the box so that the open side is down. Glue long nails or small sticks into each corner of the box for legs. Be sure that the legs are all the same length.

You may wish just to suggest a

table at the back of the stage, as you did the bridge in "The Three Billy Goats Gruff." Cut out the side view of a table. Paste it on cardboard and cut it out. Then paste it to the back edge of your stage.

ACTION

If you are using paper puppets, you

may want to use puppets that can move out onto the stage. Your puppets will not have to move out onto the stage in the first act. But you may find that puppets that can move freely are easier to use in the second act. If you wish to use this kind of puppet, follow the directions for making them in "The Princess Who Could Not Cry."

In the second act, the Dog, Cat, and the two Mice move back and forth across the stage. For this you will need two people operating the puppets. One person can move the Dog and Hiram. The other person can move the Cat and Charlie. A third person can move the Cook. Or you can use five people if you have room behind your stage for that many.

ACT 1

CHARLIE (*just coming in*): Hello! Hello! Is there anybody here?

HIRAM: Oh, it's you, Charlie. It's you,

Charlie Mouse. I've been looking for you. It's grand to see you after all these years! And how is the city?

CHARLIE: Wonderful! Wonderful! Nothing like it! You should live there, too. (*Looking around.*) This place looks about the same. It's been a long time since I was here.

HIRAM: Yes, everything is just the same. I've cleaned things up and fixed it all to look just as it did when you went to the city.

CHARLIE: Cold old place, isn't it?

HIRAM: The walls of this old barn are full of holes. They always have been. You know that.

CHARLIE: I should know. I lived here.

But those days are over. Ah, the city!

HIRAM: Let's eat while we talk. Breakfast is ready.

CHARLIE: Fine. It's a long way from the city.

HIRAM: Here you are. Wheat grains and bread crumbs. This was the breakfast you always liked best.

CHARLIE: No pancakes?

HIRAM: Pancakes? What are they? I have a few old cake crumbs if you want them.

CHARLIE (*eating crumbs*): Hard as rocks! Hiram, how can you stay

here? Cold house. Poor food. And nothing to do for fun.

HIRAM: Well, now, I have things to do that are fun. I listen to the frogs singing in the summer. And in the winter I hear the wind blowing through the trees. It is a nice sound when one is warm and safe in the barn.

CHARLIE: You don't know what fun is! The city is full of fun. Always something to do.

HIRAM: Is there?

CHARLIE: Yes, there's always something doing. And food! Why, I eat like a king at my house.

HIRAM: You make it sound wonderful.

CHARLIE: It is. It's the only place to live.

HIRAM: Someday I must go to the city and see for myself.

CHARLIE: Why not today? Come with me today.

HIRAM: But you just came here. Won't you stay awhile?

CHARLIE: In the country? No, not me! Come on, let's go.

ACT 2

CHARLIE: Here it is, Cousin Hiram. This is my house in the city.

HIRAM: Oh, it's beautiful. It's warm and clean and light.

CHARLIE: Yes, and look at the table.

HIRAM: My! I've never seen so much food.

CHARLIE: Just leftovers, Cousin. Just leftovers.

HIRAM: When do we eat?

CHARLIE: Well, let me show you around first.

HIRAM: Let's eat now. The food looks good.

CHARLIE: No, of course not. We can't jump in and eat like pigs. Not in the city.

HIRAM: I guess I'll never learn city ways.

CHARLIE: Of course you will, cousin. Now come with me. (*Stops and listens.*) No, wait a bit. I think we had better eat now.

HIRAM: But I thought you said we should wait.

CHARLIE: Don't you hear the cook in the kitchen? She'll soon be out to clear the table.

HIRAM: But you said——

CHARLIE: Never mind what I said. Eat all you can as fast as you can. And eat it now.

(MICE *hop up on table and begin to eat.*)

HIRAM: It's all very good. But why must we eat so fast?

(COOK *enters.*)

COOK: Mice on the table!

HIRAM: Who's that?

CHARLIE: The cook! The cook! Run! Run, Hiram!

COOK: The idea! Mice on the table! Just wait until I catch them.

HIRAM: Where shall I go? Where?

CHARLIE: Here, here behind the chair.

HIRAM: Don't let her catch me.

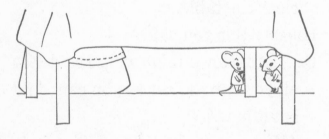

COOK: If there is anything I do not like, it is a mouse on the table.

(COOK *looks but cannot find mice. She goes out of room.*)

CHARLIE: Well, she's gone for now.

HIRAM: Are we safe?

CHARLIE: Not yet.

HIRAM: Will she come back?

CHARLIE: Yes, she'll be back. She'll bring the dog and cat to chase us.

HIRAM: Oh, no!

(DOG and CAT enter. They bark and meow as they run about the room looking for the mice.)

HIRAM: What will we do?

CHARLIE: Do? Why we'll run, of course.

(More running.)

HIRAM: Charlie, I can't run any more.

CHARLIE: I'm tired myself. So follow me.

HIRAM: What will we do?

CHARLIE: We'll lead the dog and cat onto the table.

HIRAM: Why?

CHARLIE: Keep still and watch. Do what I do. Here, nice kitty. Come on, kitty.

CAT: RRROWWW!

HIRAM: Here, puppy dog.

DOG: RROFFFFF!

(*Mice run across table.* DOG *and* CAT *follow.*)

COOK: On my table. You bad animals. Out with you. Out with you!

(COOK *chases* DOG *and* CAT *out of the room.*)

CHARLIE: Well, they are gone, and the fun is over.

HIRAM: Fun! Was that fun?

CHARLIE: Well, didn't you have fun?

HIRAM: Is this the fun you were tell-ing me about? Is this your fun in the city?

CHARLIE: Why, yes. This is what the city is like. Gay and always full of fun.

HIRAM: If that is your fun, I'm going back to the country. You may like the city, but the country has my kind of fun. The country is home to me.

Simpleton

CHARACTERS

SIMPLETON: A young man dressed in overalls. He is not really so simple. He just likes to daydream.

BROTHER: Older than Simpleton, but also dressed in overalls. He thinks a person should keep busy instead of dreaming.

MOTHER: An old woman dressed in everyday dress. She may not seem so at first, but she is really very kind.

MAN: This man wears a suit. All he cares about is making a good bargain.

FIRST DOORMAN: He is not honest.

SECOND DOORMAN: He is selfish.

KING: He is jolly, and a bit absent-minded.

SCENERY AND ACTION

You will probably find that hand puppets will be the easiest kind of puppets to use in this play. Almost all of the puppets need to hold something.

A box stage will be best for this play. But you do not need much scenery. You can use a plain board stage if you like.

Act 1 takes place in the field near Simpleton's house. He and his brother are working. Each one has a hoe or a rake. Cut a rake or a hoe out of paper. The brother holds his rake and works with it all through the act. Simpleton

just holds his. He does not work at all.

If you are using a box stage, you can make a background of a field. There can be rows of plants coming up with brown earth between.

In Act 2, Simpleton is talking to his mother. She is hanging up her washing. She may have some scraps in a small box in front of her. She is hanging up a large white piece of cloth. She may hold the cloth in the whole scene —except when she goes into the

house. Then the sheet can be on the floor. Fasten a string from one side of your stage to the other for the clothes-line.

Act 3 takes place along a road. There may be a few bushes and trees in the background. Or you may use the same scenery you used in Act 1.

In Act 3 the man has a basket with a goose in it. You can make a basket from half of a walnut shell. Fasten a piece of paper or a small wire from

one side of the shell to the other for a handle. Or you may use a small box covered with brown paper. Give the box a handle, too. Cut a goose from a piece of white paper.

In Act 4, Simpleton comes to the palace. Use a background of a large gate. The gate is locked. A man stands in front of it.

Act 4 takes place in the Throne Room. The King can be sitting in one back corner of the room. Make a throne the same way you make one for the story of "The Princess Who Could Not Cry." The King can be a paper puppet. Or he can be a hand puppet. You will have to work with the puppet and the chair until you can make it

look as though the King is sitting down.

ACT 1

SIMPLETON: What a beautiful day!

The sun is bright and yellow, and the sky is deep, deep blue.

BROTHER: Simpleton, what are you saying?

SIMPLETON: That this is a beautiful day, brother.

BROTHER: Everyone knows it's a beautiful day. We must get on with the work.

SIMPLETON: The clouds make pictures in the sky. Look, Brother! There is a whole flock of sheep.

BROTHER: We have no time for pictures in the sky. We must keep busy.

SIMPLETON: Someday I shall live in a palace. Like that one up there.

BROTHER: What palace?

SIMPLETON: Can't you see it? There it is. The clouds make high, high towers.

BROTHER: Will you please keep your mind on your work? There's so much to do.

SIMPLETON: Yes, but one day I shall live in a palace. Just you wait and see.

BROTHER: I'm waiting for you to do some work. I think you should go home and help Mother. You're no help here.

SIMPLETON: Very well. Such a blue sky! And the clouds so soft and white. One day I shall live in a palace.

(*He goes off.*)

BROTHER: Poor Simpleton. Live in a palace! Poor, simple Simpleton.

(*Let* BROTHER *go on working for a few seconds before you draw the curtain.*)

ACT 2

SIMPLETON: Isn't it a beautiful day, Mother?

MOTHER: Simpleton! Why aren't you helping your brother?

SIMPLETON: He sent me home to help you.

MOTHER: Were you dreaming again?

SIMPLETON: Just a little. Oh, look! See the cloud ship.

MOTHER: Where?

SIMPLETON: Over there. See the white sails!

MOTHER: Why, it does look like—— Simpleton! I've no time for looking at cloud pictures. Help me hang up this sheet.

SIMPLETON: (*He holds one end of the sheet.*) Oh, look at that beautiful butterfly!

MOTHER: Where?

SIMPLETON: On the bush. Over there. (*When he points he drops his end of the sheet.*)

MOTHER: Simpleton! Look what you've done! The sheet is in the dirt.

SIMPLETON: Oh, I'm sorry, Mother.

MOTHER: Now I'll have to wash it all over again. You're no help at all.

SIMPLETON: Maybe I should go out into the world and seek my fortune.

MOTHER: How would you get along in the world?

SIMPLETON: Oh, I could get by. Besides, how will I ever live in a palace if I stay here?

MOTHER: Live in a palace! I wish you'd stop saying that.

SIMPLETON: But I shall. And I shall set out to seek my fortune now.

70

MOTHER: Wait, I have a piece of silver. (*She runs in the house and
comes out with a coin.*) It isn't
much, so spend it wisely, my son.

SIMPLETON: Thank you, Mother. And,
don't worry about me.

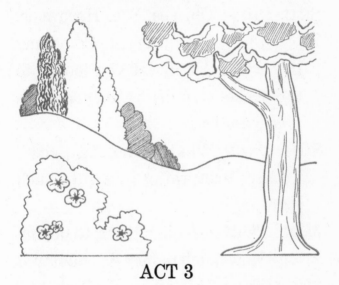

ACT 3

(*The countryside. Simpleton meets a
man with a big covered basket.*)

SIMPLETON: Isn't it a beautiful day?

MAN: It's fair enough.

SIMPLETON: What have you on your
arm?

MAN: I have a basket, you simpleton.
Can't you see that?

SIMPLETON: Of course I see the basket. But what do you have in it?

MAN: That is none of your business.

SIMPLETON: And that is too bad. I'm looking for something to buy.

MAN: Have you any money?

SIMPLETON: Oh, yes. See. Here it is.

MAN: Oh, that's different. Come, my boy. I will gladly let you look into my basket. (*He lifts the cover. The goose honks.*)

SIMPLETON: What a fine, fat goose! I'd give everything I own for such a goose.

MAN: That's a foolish thing to do, my boy. How much money do you have?

SIMPLETON: This piece of silver.

MAN: A fair price for the goose.

SIMPLETON: Your silver. (*He gives the silver to the man.*)

MAN: Your goose. (*He gives Simpleton the basket.*)

SIMPLETON: Sir, which way is it to the King's palace?

MAN: Right down this road. Why do you ask?

SIMPLETON: I'm going to take this goose to the King.

MAN: You spent all your money for the goose, and now you're going to give it away? Silly boy. Ho, ho, ho!

SIMPLETON: Laugh if you like. But one day I shall live in a palace. Just you wait and see.

MAN: Silly boy. Ho, ho, ho! Silly Simpleton. Ho, ho, ho!

ACT 4

(*Palace of the King. Simpleton walks in, and a doorman comes in and stops him.*)

FIRST DOORMAN: Stop! No one enters.

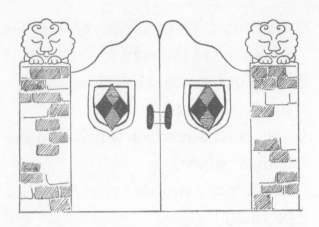

SIMPLETON: I want to see the King. I want to give him this fine goose.

FIRST DOORMAN: A goose? Let me see it.

SIMPLETON: Isn't it a beauty? (*He lifts the cover. The goose honks.*)

FIRST DOORMAN: If you will give me half the goose, you may see the King.

SIMPLETON: I cannot give the King only half a goose.

FIRST DOORMAN: The King is very kind. He will give you a bag of gold or silver. Say that you will give me half of what the King gives to you. Then I will let you see him.

SIMPLETON: Oh, I will gladly give you

half of what the King gives me.
Now may I go in?

FIRST DOORMAN: Second Doorman!

(*He goes out.*)

SECOND DOORMAN: Who are you?

SIMPLETON: I want to see the King. I
want to give him this goose.

SECOND DOORMAN: What goose?

SIMPLETON: The goose in my basket.
(*He lifts the cover. The goose
honks.*)

SECOND DOORMAN: You may see the
King if you will give me half of
what the King gives you for the
goose.

SIMPLETON: But I have already said
that I will give half of what I get
to the other doorman.

SECOND DOORMAN: Unless you give me half, you cannot see the King.

SIMPLETON: But I must see the King! Very well, I'll give you the other half.

SECOND DOORMAN: Then you may go in.

ACT 5

SIMPLETON: Your Majesty! (*He bows to the King.*)

KING: What have we here?

SIMPLETON: A gift for you, sir.

KING: Dear me. What is it?

SIMPLETON: See for yourself. (*He*

lifts the cover. The goose honks.)

KING: A goose! A fine, fat, feathery goose! You're a fine, fat boy——I mean, you're a fine, noble lad to give it to me. I am very pleased. I would like to give you something.

SIMPLETON: You are very kind, Your Majesty.

KING: Would you like a fine, fat, feathery—I mean, a fine horse?

SIMPLETON: No. No thank you, sir.

KING: I know! A fine, fat house!

SIMPLETON: No thank you, sir.

KING: Money? Everybody likes money—fine, fat or otherwise.

SIMPLETON: No. That is not what I

should like. The thing I should like
is a beating.

KING: A beating! You want a beating?

SIMPLETON: That is what I want. A
good beating.

KING: If that is what you want, you
shall have it. I'll call my biggest
guards. But why do you want a
beating?

SIMPLETON: Your two doormen
wouldn't let me in. I had to say that
I would give each one half of what
you would give me.

KING: Oho! So that's it! And they
shall get the beating they asked for.
And they will no longer be my doormen. What is your name, my boy?

SIMPLETON: Everyone calls me Simpleton. I'm always saying that one
day I shall live in a palace.

KING: Simpleton, is it? You are not so
simple. And you shall live in a palace. You will be my doorman. I
know you will be fair to those who

come to see the King.

SIMPLETON: Oh, thank you, sir. Shall
I begin now?

KING: In time, my boy. First you will
dine with the King upon a fine, fat,
feathery goose!

The Little Red Hen

CHARACTERS

MISS HEN: She is a neat little red hen. She wears an apron.

MR. RACCOON: A fat, lazy raccoon.

MR. RABBIT: A fat white rabbit. He is just as lazy as Mr. Raccoon.

MR. SQUIRREL: A fat red squirrel. He, too, is lazy.

SCENERY AND ACTION

You will want to use a box stage for this play. Acts 1 through 6 take place outside of Miss Hen's house.

Build a house in one corner of the stage. The front of the house should face the opening in the floor of the stage that the puppets come through. The side of the house should face the front of the stage and the audience. Find a square cardboard box the right size for your house. Use only the top or the bottom of the box. Place the box with the open part over the opening in the stage. Draw some windows on the side that faces the audience. Draw a door on the side of the house that faces the opening in the floor of the stage. Cut along one side and the top of the door. Now the door will open and the puppets can go in and out of the house.

The scenery behind the house and

on the stage should suggest a yard.

In Act 4 Miss Hen should be looking at her wheat coming up. A small strip of green paper fastened to the stage will make a fine wheat plant.

In Act 5 Miss Hen is looking at her wheat plant again. This time the plant is larger. Use a little longer strip of green paper.

In Act 6 the wheat plant is cut down. Miss Hen should be holding it.

Acts 7 and 8 take place inside of the house. Make a few chairs like the throne suggested in "The Princess Who Could Not Cry." The scenery on the back wall of the stage should show a kitchen with a stove. Draw your own kitchen, or cut pictures from maga-

zines and paste them on a piece of
paper to make your scenery.

In Act 7 Miss Hen should be holding
a small white bag. Make a bag by cut-
ting a round piece of white cloth. Sew

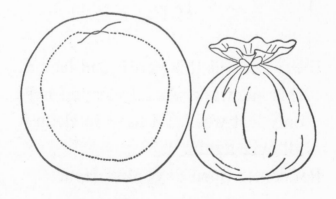

all around the edge of the cloth. Pull the thread tight so that a bag is made. Fasten the thread.

In Act 8 Miss Hen has a loaf of bread. Cut a loaf out of paper. Or use a piece of wood the shape of a loaf of bread.

You will want to use a hand puppet for Miss Hen. The other puppets can be paper puppets. Or they can be hand puppets, too.

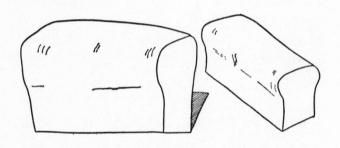

ACT 1

HEN: Look at this yard! And look at this sidewalk! And I cleaned here only last week. I'll have to clean it all over again.

RACCOON: Good day, Miss Hen.

HEN: Good day, Mr. Raccoon.

RACCOON: Nice place you have here.

HEN: Why, thank you.

RACCOON: You know, I've been looking for a place to stay.

HEN: You have?

RACCOON: Yes. And I think your
house is just what I've been looking
for.

HEN: But, Mr. Raccoon, I——

RACCOON: Yes, I think I'm going to
like it here. (*He goes inside.*)

HEN: Well! I'm not running a board-
inghouse.

RABBIT: Hello, Miss Hen.

HEN: Hello, Mr. Rabbit.

RABBIT: Nice place you have here.

HEN: Why, that's what Mr. Raccoon said.

RABBIT: You know, I'm looking for a place to stay.

HEN: Now, wait a minute, Mr. Rabbit. I'm not——

RABBIT: Now, now, Miss Hen, you don't have to beg me. I'll be glad to move in.

HEN: But I'm not running a——

RABBIT: Lovely place. (*He goes inside.*)

HEN: Oh, dear! What will I do with two boarders—Mr. Raccoon and Mr. Rabbit? I tried to tell them that I'm not running a——oh! Good day, Mr. Squirrel.

SQUIRREL: Hello there, Miss Hen. My, my, you have a nice place here. It's as nice as it can be.

HEN: Now, Mr. Squirrel, if you're looking for a place to stay——

SQUIRREL: Do you mean that I can move right in?

86

HEN: That's not what I was going to say.

SQUIRREL: I'd love to stay here. I hear that you're a good cook, too.

HEN: I can't cook for three of you!

SQUIRREL: Three! You mean you have two other boarders? Good! I'll have someone to talk to.

HEN: Oh dear. You just can't move into my house.

SQUIRREL: No trouble at all. No trouble at all. You'll be surprised at how quickly I can make myself at home. (*He goes inside.*)

HEN: Oh dear. I came out to clean my yard, and now I have three boarders. Whatever will I do?

87

ACT 2 (*Two weeks later.*)

RACCOON: Miss Hen, I don't like to say this, but we've had corn three times a day for the past week.

HEN: I'm sorry that you don't like corn, Mr. Raccoon. I'm a hen, and all hens love corn. That's all I have to eat.

RACCOON: Well, if you don't feed us anything but corn, I may have to move.

HEN: We could have something different if you'd get it. All you do is sit around and talk with Mr. Rabbit.

RACCOON: Really, Miss Hen, it's none of your business what your boarders do.

HEN: It is when my boarders don't pay me any board. Just when are you going to——

RACCOON: I'm sorry, Miss Hen, but I think I hear Mr. Squirrel calling. (*He goes off.*)

'HEN: Every time I say something about money, they hear someone calling. But maybe he is right about the corn. I'm going for a walk. Perhaps I'll find a patch of greens for salad. La la la. (*She goes off.*)

ACT 3 (*A little while later*)

HEN (*She runs up to house with a grain of wheat.*): Mr. Raccoon! Come quickly, Mr. Raccoon!

RACCOON: What is it, Miss Hen? Do you have some ice cream for me?

HEN: No, I have a grain of wheat. I found it on my walk in the country.

RACCOON: A grain of wheat? I don't want a grain of wheat.

HEN: I don't want to give it to you.

I want you to help me plant it.

RACCOON: Help you plant it! I have other things to do besides planting a grain of wheat. (*He goes off.*)

HEN: Oh dear. Mr. Rabbit! Come here Mr. Rabbit!

RABBIT: Yes?

HEN: I have a grain of wheat.

RABBIT: Just throw it down. No one will ever see it.

HEN: The very idea! I want you to help me plant it.

RABBIT: Plant it! Whatever for? I have other things to do. Plant a grain of wheat, indeed! (*He goes off.*)

HEN: Well, there's Mr. Squirrel left.

Mr. Squirrel! Can you come out?

SQUIRREL: Is lunch ready?

HEN: No, Mr. Squirrel. I want you to help me plant this grain of wheat.

SQUIRREL: Plant a grain of wheat! What a waste of time. I have other things to do. (*He goes off.*)

HEN: Really! Well, I suppose I'll have to plant the grain of wheat myself. La la la.

ACT 4 (*Weeks later*)

HEN: We've surely had dry weather. My wheat needs watering. And I've so much to do. Oh, Mr. Raccoon!

RACCOON: Are you calling me, Miss Hen?

HEN: Yes, Mr. Raccoon. I wonder if you'd help me. My wheat needs watering.

RACCOON: Are you asking me to come out in the hot sun just to water that wheat?

HEN: It's very dry.

RACCOON: If it wants water, let it water itself.

HEN: That's a silly thing to say.

RACCOON: Well, I'm not coming out in that hot sun. I might get freckles. (*He goes off.*)

HEN: Whoever heard of a raccoon with freckles? Mr. Rabbit!

RABBIT: Yes, Miss Hen?

HEN: Would you help me water my wheat?

RABBIT: What! Come out in the sunshine? Why, I'd get sunburned. My ears would peel.

HEN: You wouldn't have to be out that long.

RABBIT: No, no. I really can't. (*He goes off.*)

HEN: You'd think I had asked him to walk five miles to get the water. Mr. Squirrel!

SQUIRREL: Such hot weather!

HEN: Would you mind helping me water my wheat?

SQUIRREL: In this sun! Do you want

me to get sick? No, indeed. I will not help you. (*He goes off.*)

HEN: Well, I guess I'll have to water the wheat myself.

ACT 5 (*Harvest Time*)

HEN: My wheat is ripe. Oh, Mr. Raccoon!

RACCOON: Yes, Miss Hen?

HEN: Will you help me cut my wheat?

RACCOON: I'm sorry Miss Hen, but I'm busy.

HEN: Mr. Rabbit, will you help me cut my wheat?

RABBIT: Sorry, but I have a great many things to do.

HEN: Mr. Squirrel, will you help me cut my wheat?

SQUIRREL: Heavens, no! I'm busy talking to Mr. Rabbit.

HEN: Then I'll have to cut the wheat myself.

ACT 6 (*An hour later*)

HEN: It's time to take my wheat to the mill to be ground. Mr. Raccoon, will you help me take my wheat to the mill?

RACCOON: I should say not.

HEN: Mr. Rabbit?

RABBIT: No, of course not!

HEN: Mr. Squirrel?

SQUIRREL: Indeed not!

HEN: Then I will take the wheat to the mill for grinding myself.

ACT 7

HEN: Now I have flour from my wheat. Who will help me make the bread?

RACCOON: I don't have time to make bread.

RABBIT: Nor do I.

SQUIRREL: Let someone else make the bread.

HEN: Very well, I'll make the bread myself.

ACT 8 (*Dinner time*)

RACCOON: What do I smell?

RABBIT: It smells so good!

SQUIRREL: Oh, it smells wonderful!

HEN: It's the bread I made from my wheat.

RACCOON: Miss Hen, I will gladly help you eat the bread.

RABBIT: So will I.

SQUIRREL: And I, too.

HEN: Ho! Ho! You all want to eat the

bread. But you wouldn't help me plant the wheat. You wouldn't help water it. You wouldn't help me cut it, or take it to the mill, or make the bread.

THE THREE: But we're so hungry.

HEN: You're lazy. I've put up with the three of you as long as I can. Out you go! Where's my broom? (*She chases them with her broom.*)

THE THREE: Don't hit us! We're going! (*They run off.*)

HEN: Now I can eat my bread in peace. Ah, I do believe it was worth all the work. Never have I eaten better bread!